WHOSE POO?

POO IN THE FOREST

by

Emilie Dufresne

BEARPORT
PUBLISHING

Minneapolis, Minnesota

Credits:

All images are courtesy of Shutterstock.com, unless otherwise specified. With thanks to Getty Images, Thinkstock Photo, and iStockphoto. Front Cover - PremiumVector, ainahart, Svietlieisha Olena, Evlakhov Valeriy, Ewoka. Title typeface used throughout - PremiumVector. 2 - picturepartners. 4 - dugdax, ideyweb. 5 - Doug McLean. 6 - RedlineVector. 6&7 - Corrado Trelanzi. 7 - Denis Tabler, Ekaterina V. Borisova, photomaster. 8 - Bob Hilscher, Top Vector Studio. 9 - Victor.A. 10&11 - FCG, VectorKnight. 11 - Eric Isselee, LazyFocus, Svetlana Foote, Mascha Tace. 12 - Allison Coffin. 13 - Lillian Tveit, olgasoi007, Yev0. 14 - notkoo. 14&15 - Matyas Rehak. 15 - Gallinago_media, Martin Mecnarowski, tristan tan. 16 - robuart, beeboys. 17 - icosha, art.tkach. 18 - VectorShow. 18&19 - Anneli Salo [CC BY-SA 4.0 (https://creativecommons.org/licenses/by-sa/4.0). 19 - Eric Isselee, Galushko Sergey, Inspiring, IrinaK, Moomchak V. Design. 20 - Mr. SUTTIPON YAKHAM. 21 - Moomchak V. Design, Magicleaf, benchart, vbnzqcthutd. 22 - duangnapa_b, remart, notkoo. 22&23 - Dr Morley Read.

Library of Congress Cataloging-in-Publication Data

Names: Dufresne, Emilie, author.
Title: Poo in the forest / by Emilie Dufresne.
Description: Fusion. | Minneapolis, Minnesota : Bearport Publishing, [2021]
 | Series: Whose poo? | Includes bibliographical references and index.
Identifiers: LCCN 2020009331 (print) | LCCN 2020009332 (ebook) | ISBN
 9781647473839 (library binding) | ISBN 9781647473884 (paperback) | ISBN
 9781647473938 (ebook)
Subjects: LCSH: Forests and forestry--Juvenile literature. | Feces--v
 Juvenile literature.
Classification: LCC QH86 .D84 2021 (print) | LCC QH86 (ebook) | DDC
 333.75--dc23
LC record available at https://lccn.loc.gov/2020009331
LC ebook record available at https://lccn.loc.gov/2020009332

For more information, write to Bearport Publishing, 5357 Penn Avenue South, Minneapolis, MN 55419. Printed in the United States of America.

CONTENTS

ALL ABOUT POO

Let's take a look at forests all over the world and see who has been pooing in them.

Don't touch any poo you find in the forest. Poo has a lot of nasty things in it!

On the next pages, you will see poo in the forest. Learn all about that poo and think about which animal made it. Then, turn the page to see if you were right.

WET AND SEEDY

Look at this huge poo! Whose poo could it be?

There are seeds in this poo. The animal must eat a lot of berries.

This poo is very runny. It is a purple-black color.

Whose poo could this be?
Choose which of these three
animals you think did it.

Deer

It is a large poo, so it probably came from a larger animal.

Wolf

Do I look like I eat berries?

There are some green bits in this poo. This animal has also been eating plants.

Bear

WHOSE POO WAS IT?

It was the **bear's POO!**

I think I bit my tongue!

Bears will eat what they can get their paws on.

In summer, bears eat a lot of berries. The seeds end up in their poo.

Bear poo might have plants, seeds, hair, or bones in it.

The poo might be a green color if the bear has been eating more plants.

9

HARD AND HAIRY

Is this a poo or a hair ball?

This poo is stinky. This animal probably eats a lot of meat.

This poo is full of hair.

Whose poo could this be? Choose which of these three animals you think did it.

This poo has bits of bones in it. This animal probably eats other animals.

Fox

Wolf

How much do you think I eat?

Squirrel

The poo is a similar shape and size to dog poo, so it might come from a dog-like animal.

WHOSE POO WAS IT?

It was the
**wolf's
POO!**

Awhooooo! I am the one that made the furry poo.

Wolf poo is partly made up of the hair and bones of **prey** they have eaten.

Hair and bones are very hard to **digest**, so they come out looking very similar to how they went in.

Wolf poo smells bad because of all the meat in a wolf's diet.

The smell of a wolf's poo also helps it mark its **territory**.

PILES OF PELLETS

Look at these tiny piles of poo. Whose could they be?

These **pellets** are dry and hard.

Usually **rodents** make small, pellet-shaped poo.

Whose poo could this be? Choose which of these three animals you think did it.

Capybara

There are lots of piles of poo, so this animal probably lives in a group.

Badger

This poo looks very smooth, so the food has been well digested.

I wish my poo was that small.

Moose

15

WHOSE POO WAS IT?

It was the
capybara's
POO!

Yum! Yum!
It's time for my
favorite food.

Capybaras make two
different types of poo. They
eat one of these types!

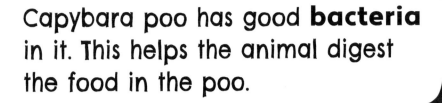

Capybara poo has good **bacteria** in it. This helps the animal digest the food in the poo.

The second time this poo comes out, it looks like small, hard pellets.

Capybaras can eat about 6.6 pounds (3 kg) of grass a day. That is about the same weight as four loaves of bread.

17

SMALL, SLIMY, AND SHINY

Don't miss this poo. It is so small!
Whose slimy **scat** is that?

This poo has bits of bugs.
This animal must eat
beetles and other insects.

This poo is a very dark color.

WHOSE POO WAS IT?

It was the **hedgehog's** POO!

Hedgehogs eat a lot of different critters. Sometimes a bug wing or leg can be seen in hedgehog poo.

If a hedgehog has eaten a lot of slugs and snails, its poo can be slimy!

Sluurrrp! Slimy slugs are my favorite.

Hedgehog poo can be as long as 2 inches (5 cm). That's a little smaller than an eraser.

21

BONUS POO!

WAIT, THAT'S NOT POO!

This owl pellet might look like poo on the forest floor, but it isn't! However, it is what an owl ate.

They look like a tasty dinner!

Owls eat small creatures such as mice, voles, and sometimes frogs.

Owls swallow their food whole. But they can't digest every part of the animals they eat. Some parts such as bone and hair don't get digested.

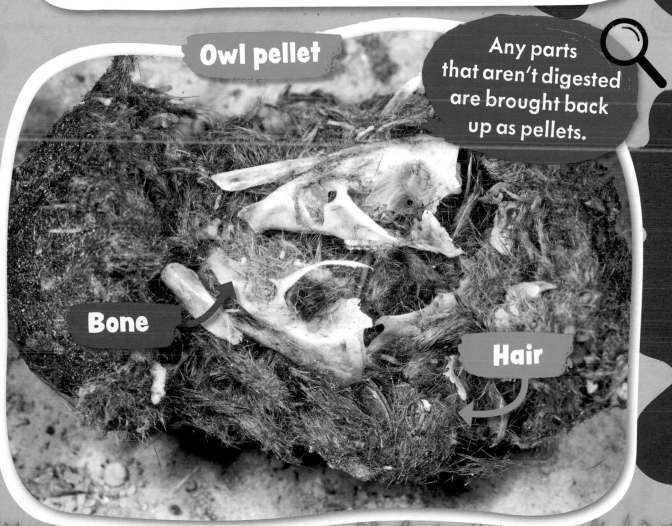

Owl pellet

Any parts that aren't digested are brought back up as pellets.

Bone

Hair

GLOSSARY

bacteria tiny living things, too small to see, that live inside animals

diet what an animal eats

digested to have broken down food into things that can be used by the body

pellets small, hard balls of poop or undigested food

prey animals that are eaten by other animals for food

rodents animals such as rats and mice that have four feet and have long front teeth used for gnawing and nibbling

scat animal poo

territory the area where an animal lives and finds food

INDEX